D0722206

SEP 14

Texas

Explore the United States

Sarah Tieck

Big Buddy BOOKS
Explore the United States

VISIT US AT
www.abdopublishing.com

Published by ABDO Publishing Company, PO Box 398166, Minneapolis, MN 55439.

Printed in the United States of America, North Mankato, Minnesota.
052012
092012

♻ PRINTED ON RECYCLED PAPER

Coordinating Series Editor: Rochelle Baltzer
Contributing Editors: Megan M. Gunderson, Marcia Zappa
Graphic Design: Adam Craven
Cover Photograph: *Shutterstock*: ssuaphotos.
Interior Photographs/Illustrations: *Alamy*: Aurora Photos (p. 26); *AP Photo*: The Lufkin Daily News, Joel Andrews (p. 27), AP Photo (p. 23), J. Scott Applewhite (p. 25), Cal Sports Media via AP Images (p. 21); *Getty Images*: Carolyn Brown (p. 11), Kean Collection (p. 13), Rick Wilking (p. 25); *iStockphoto*: ©iStockphoto.com/codyphotography (p. 5), ©iStockphoto.com/egearing (p. 17), ©iStockphoto.com/ericfoltz (p. 29), ©iStockphoto.com/pelicankate (p. 30); *Shutterstock*: Steve Byland (p. 30), cholder (p. 19), Jeffrey M. Frank (p. 27), Randy Heich (p. 30), David Huntley (p. 9), Philip Lange (p. 30), Mike Norton (p. 26), Jim Parkin (p. 19), Brandon Seidel (pp. 9, 11, 27).

All population figures taken from the 2010 US census.

Library of Congress Cataloging-in-Publication Data

Tieck, Sarah, 1976-
 Texas / Sarah Tieck.
   p. cm. -- (Explore the United States)
 ISBN 978-1-61783-382-3
 1. Texas--Juvenile literature. I. Title.
 F386.3.T47 2013
 976.4--dc23
                        2012017231

Contents

ONE NATION

The United States is a **diverse** country. It has farmland, cities, coasts, and mountains. Its people come from many different backgrounds. And, its history covers more than 200 years.

Today the country includes 50 states. Texas is one of these states. Let's learn more about Texas and its story!

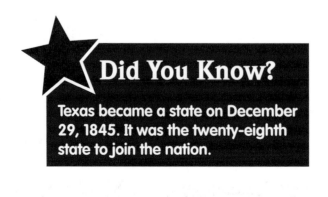

Did You Know?

Texas became a state on December 29, 1845. It was the twenty-eighth state to join the nation.

Texas is known for cattle ranches (*above*) and oil wells.

TEXAS UP CLOSE

The United States has four main **regions**. Texas is in the South.

Texas has four states on its borders. Oklahoma is north and east. Arkansas is northeast and Louisiana is east. New Mexico is west and north. The Gulf of Mexico is southeast. The country of Mexico is southwest.

Texas is the second-largest state in size and population. It has a total area of 266,833 square miles (691,094 sq km). About 25 million people live in Texas.

REGIONS OF THE UNITED STATES

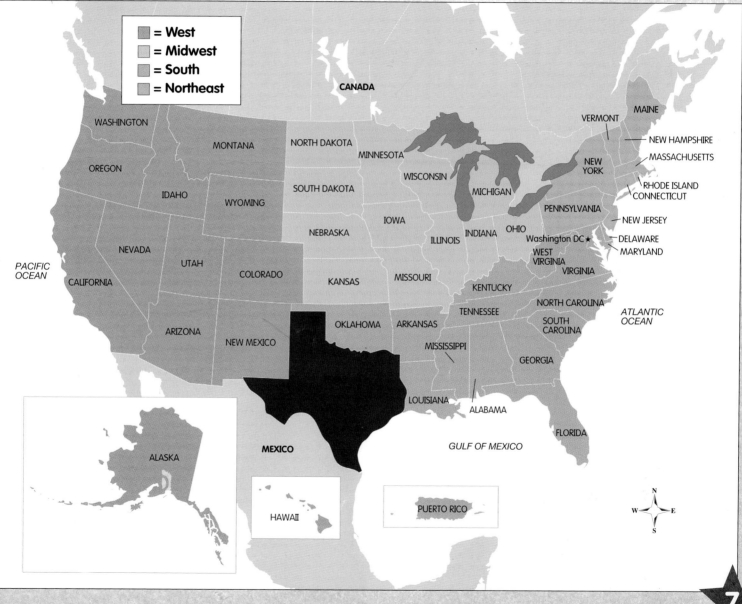

= West
= Midwest
= South
= Northeast

CANADA

WASHINGTON
OREGON
IDAHO
MONTANA
NORTH DAKOTA
MINNESOTA
WISCONSIN
MICHIGAN
VERMONT
MAINE
NEW HAMPSHIRE
MASSACHUSETTS
NEW YORK
RHODE ISLAND
CONNECTICUT
NEVADA
UTAH
WYOMING
SOUTH DAKOTA
IOWA
NEBRASKA
ILLINOIS
INDIANA
OHIO
PENNSYLVANIA
NEW JERSEY
DELAWARE
MARYLAND
WEST VIRGINIA
VIRGINIA
Washington DC ★
CALIFORNIA
COLORADO
KANSAS
MISSOURI
KENTUCKY
NORTH CAROLINA
ARIZONA
NEW MEXICO
OKLAHOMA
ARKANSAS
TENNESSEE
SOUTH CAROLINA
MISSISSIPPI
GEORGIA
LOUISIANA
ALABAMA
FLORIDA

PACIFIC OCEAN
ATLANTIC OCEAN
GULF OF MEXICO

ALASKA
MEXICO
HAWAII
PUERTO RICO

N
W   E
S

IMPORTANT CITIES

Austin is the **capital** of Texas. It is located on the Colorado River. This city is the state's education center. The University of Texas is there, along with several other schools.

Houston is the largest city in Texas. It is home to 2,099,451 people. It is known for oil production and has many oil **refineries**. Also, astronauts train in Houston at Johnson Space Center.

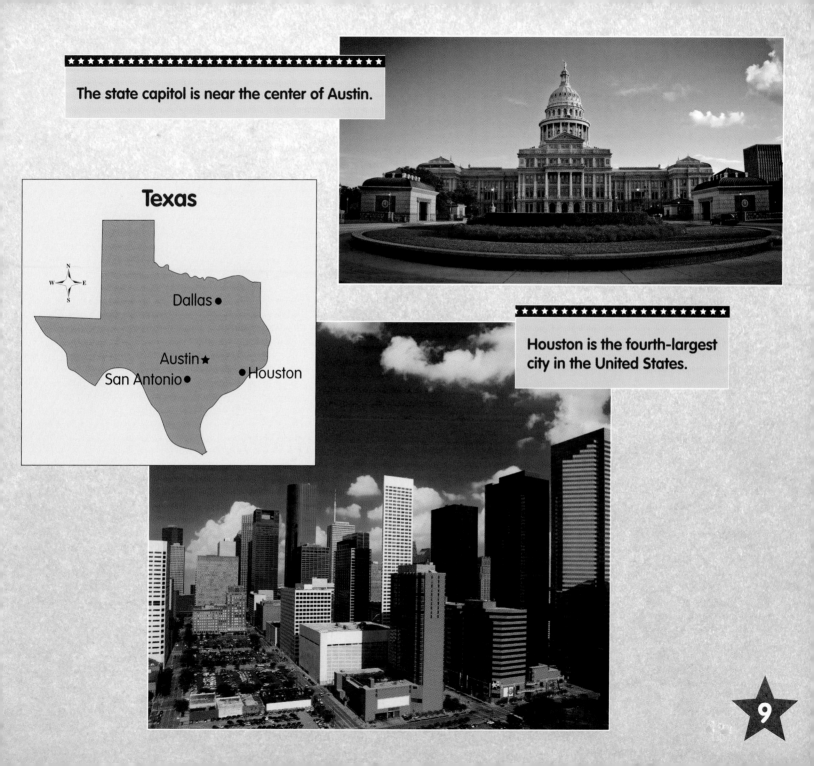

The state capitol is near the center of Austin.

Texas

Dallas •

Austin ★
San Antonio • • Houston

Houston is the fourth-largest city in the United States.

9

San Antonio is the second-largest city in Texas. It is home to 1,327,407 people. This city is known for its beauty and its history. The famous Battle of the Alamo took place there in 1836.

Dallas is the state's third-largest city, with 1,197,816 people. It is on the banks of the Trinity River. Many businesses are based in this city.

The River Walk is a famous shopping and dining area in San Antonio.

The Dallas/Fort Worth International Airport is one of the nation's busiest airports.

TEXAS IN HISTORY

The history of Texas includes Native Americans, explorers, and war. Spanish explorers arrived in the 1500s. They met Native Americans, who had lived there many years. The Spanish wanted to share their religion. So in 1682, they began building **missions**.

Over time, more settlers arrived. In 1821, Mexico won its independence from Spain. Texas was part of this new country. In 1836, Texans won the Texas Revolution. This gave them independence from Mexico. Texas became a state in 1845.

The Battle of the Alamo was an important event in the Texas Revolution.

Timeline

1821

Texas became part of the new country of Mexico.

1845

Texas became a state on December 29.

1901

A large amount of oil was discovered near Beaumont. This sparked the oil business in Texas. Many oil companies were formed.

1800s

1836

Texans and Mexicans fought in the Battle of the Alamo. A little over one month later, Texas won its independence.

1866

The first oil well in Texas was drilled near Nacogdoches.

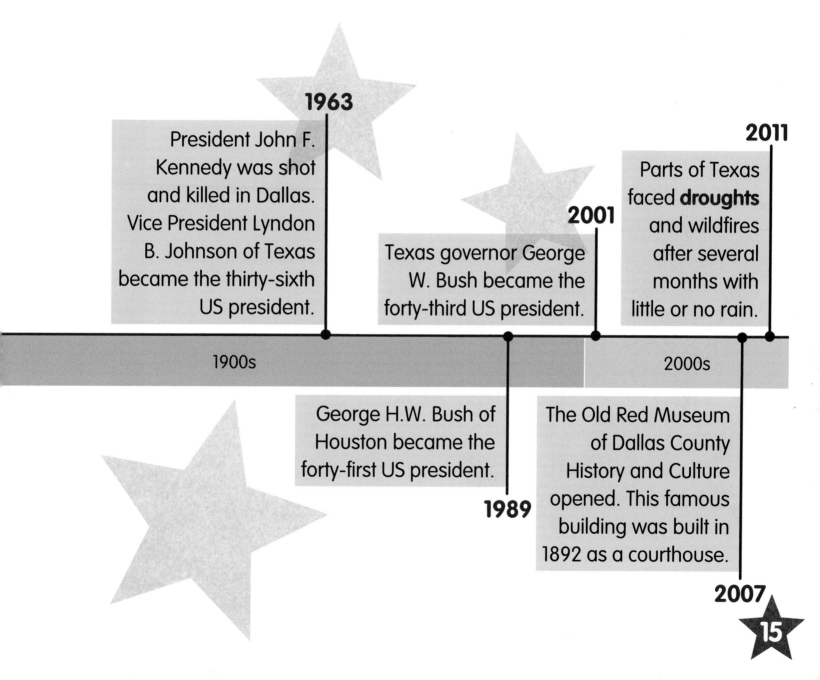

1963

President John F. Kennedy was shot and killed in Dallas. Vice President Lyndon B. Johnson of Texas became the thirty-sixth US president.

2001

Texas governor George W. Bush became the forty-third US president.

2011

Parts of Texas faced **droughts** and wildfires after several months with little or no rain.

1900s

2000s

George H.W. Bush of Houston became the forty-first US president.

1989

The Old Red Museum of Dallas County History and Culture opened. This famous building was built in 1892 as a courthouse.

2007

15

Across the Land

Texas has **plains**, rivers, forests, coasts, hills, and mountains. Major rivers include the Rio Grande and the Red River. The Gulf of Mexico forms the state's southeastern coast. And, western Texas has small mountain ranges that are part of the Rocky Mountains.

Many types of animals make their homes in Texas. These include armadillos, alligators, deer, and coyotes. Crabs, oysters, and shrimps live in the coastal waters.

Did You Know?

In July, the average temperature in Texas is 83°F (28°C). In January, it is 46°F (8°C).

Texas plains are covered with grasses and wildflowers, such as bluebonnets.

Earning a Living

Many large businesses are based in Texas. One of the US government's largest banks is located there. And, **chemicals** and food products are made in the state.

Texas has many natural **resources**. Oil, coal, salt, and other useful products come from its land. The state's farms produce livestock, wheat, corn, fruits, nuts, hay, and rice.

Texas leads the country in oil production.

Texas has different types of soil. So, a variety of crops grow in the state. These include cotton (*right*), pecans, melons, and grapefruit.

19

Sports Page

Many people think of football when they think of Texas. This state is home to the Dallas Cowboys and the Houston Texans. Texas A&M University and the University of Texas at Austin have popular college teams.

Texas also has soccer, hockey, baseball, and basketball teams. Famous baseball pitcher Nolan Ryan was born in Refugio. He played for two Texas teams during his almost 30-year career.

The University of Texas at Austin Longhorns football team is well known.

HOMETOWN HEROES

Many famous people have lived in Texas. Lyndon B. Johnson was born near Stonewall in 1908. He grew up in Johnson City.

In 1961, Johnson became vice president under President John F. Kennedy. In 1963, Kennedy was shot and killed. Then, Johnson became president. He proved a strong leader during this sad time. In 1964, he was elected for a full term.
He served until 1969.

Did You Know?

While Johnson was president, the United States was fighting in the Vietnam War. Many people didn't want the country to keep fighting in the war. This caused problems within the nation.

Johnson was the thirty-sixth US president.

23

Did You Know?

Bush is the son of the forty-first US president, George H.W. Bush.

George W. Bush was born in Connecticut in 1946. But, he grew up in Midland and Houston.

Bush became the governor of Texas in 1995. From 2001 to 2009, he served as the forty-third US president. He led the country after the **terrorist** attacks on September 11, 2001. The nation faced war and other problems while Bush was president.

Bush and his wife, Laura, set up programs to help children read.

The Bushes often visit their ranch in Crawford.

25

Tour Book

Do you want to go to Texas? If you visit the state, here are some places to go and things to do!

★ Play

Splash in the Gulf of Mexico. Padre Island National Seashore is in southern Texas. It has about 70 miles (110 km) of sandy beaches.

★ Look

Watch boats race! The Texas Water Safari is considered one of the toughest boat races. It covers 261 miles (420 km)! Part of the race is through white-water rapids. It has taken place every June since 1963.

★ Remember

Visit the historic Alamo in San Antonio. The Alamo is an old mission. It is where the Battle of the Alamo was fought.

★ Cheer

Go to a rodeo! Many Texans consider rodeo to be the state sport.

★ Discover

Explore the land in Big Bend National Park. This park is in southwestern Texas. It includes the Rio Grande, mountains, and desert land.

A GREAT STATE

The story of Texas is important to the United States. The people and places that make up this state offer something special to the country. Together with all the states, Texas helps make the United States great.

The Rio Grande is on the border between Texas and Mexico. It is one of North America's longest rivers.

Fast Facts

Date of Statehood:
December 29, 1845

State Capital:
Austin

Postal Abbreviation:
TX

Population (rank):
25,145,561
(2nd most-populated state)

Flag:

Tree: Pecan

Total Area (rank):
266,833 square miles
(2nd largest state)

Motto:
Friendship

Nickname:
Lone Star State

Flower: Bluebonnet

Bird: Northern Mockingbird

Important Words

capital a city where government leaders meet.

chemical (KEH-mih-kuhl) a substance that can cause reactions and changes.

diverse made up of things that are different from each other.

drought (DRAUT) a long period of dry weather.

mission a place where religious work is done.

plains flat or rolling land without trees.

refinery a place where unwanted parts of something are removed to make it usable.

region a large part of a country that is different from other parts.

resource a supply of something useful or valued.

terrorist a person who uses violence to scare or control people or governments.

Web Sites

To learn more about Texas, visit ABDO Publishing Company online. Web sites about Texas are featured on our Book Links page. These links are routinely monitored and updated to provide the most current information available.

www.abdopublishing.com

Index